PARANORMAL HANDBOOKS

HANDBOOK TO

UFOs, CROP CIRCLES AND ALIEN ENCOUNTERS

BY SEAN McCOLLUM

raintree

a Capstone company — publishers for children

Raintree is an imprint of Capstone Global Library Limited, a company incorporated in England and Wales having its registered office at 264 Banbury Road, Oxford, OX2 7DY – Registered company number: 6695582

www.raintree.co.uk
myorders@raintree.co.uk

Edited by Nate LeBoutillier
Designed by Philippa Jenkins
Picture research by Svetlana Zhurkin
Production by Kathy McColley
Printed and bound in China

ISBN 978 1 4747 2406 7
20 19 18 17 16
10 9 8 7 6 5 4 3 2 1

British Library Cataloguing in Publication Data
A full catalogue record for this book is available from the British Library.

Acknowledgements
We would like to thank the following for permission to reproduce photographs: Alamy: Erin Paul Donovan, 21 (bottom); Dreamstime: Michele Cornelius, cover (top), 1; iStockphoto: italiansight, cover (bottom), back cover, 15; Mary Evans Picture Library, 9 (bottom), 11, Michael Buhler, 23; Newscom: Album/Columbia Pictures, 27, Beitia Archives Digital Press Photos, 26, Mirrorpix, 7, Reuters/Mike Blake, 9 (top), Rex, 18 (top), Rex/South West News Service, 16, Rex/Steve Alexander, 18 (bottom), 19, Splash News/Solent News, 13, ZUMA Press/Dmitry Dubikovskiy, 6; Shutterstock: Arturo Escorza Pedraza, 5, Chris Harvey, 21 (top), EKS, 3, Giordano Aita, 17, Lena_graphics, 29, M. Cornelius, 28, MWaits, 8, Phil McDonald, 4, Photobank gallery, 25, Zack Frank, 22; U.S. Navy Photo by Mass Communication Specialist Seaman Andrew Skipworth, 12

Design Elements by Shutterstock

CONTENTS

VISITORS FROM OUTER SPACE 4

CHAPTER 1   MYSTERIES IN THE SKIES 6

CHAPTER 2   THE PUZZLE OF CROP CIRCLES 14

CHAPTER 3   TALES OF CLOSE ENCOUNTERS 20

CHAPTER 4   IS THE TRUTH OUT THERE? 26

HANDBOOK QUIZ 29

GLOSSARY 30

READ MORE 31

INDEX 32

Visitors from outer space

In the early morning hours of 24 July 1948, a passenger plane was cruising high over Alabama, USA. The two pilots saw a red glow in the distance. At first they thought it was an approaching jet. Then something blasted past them. It let loose a burst of flame and instantly shot into the clouds and disappeared.

The pilots were stunned. They reported the sighting to the US military. They described the object as "a wingless aircraft". It was unlike any plane or jet they had ever seen. The Air Force investigated. Scientists could only guess what it might have been. Some concluded it was a type of meteor.

The military started a study of these unidentified flying objects, or UFOs. Some experts even wondered if they might be spaceships from other worlds.

The idea that alien astronauts might visit our planet has gripped us Earthlings for decades. It is a popular topic in science-fiction books, films and TV series. It fuels our fascination with crop circles and other mysterious phenomena.

People tend to wonder: *Are we alone in the galaxy?*
UFO hunters of every kind are searching land, sky and
space for answers.

CHAPTER 1

MYSTERIES IN THE SKIES

UFO-shaped clouds over Chile

To many people, the term "UFO" suggests a spacecraft from another planet. But a UFO can be any unexplained object in the sky. Most are eventually revealed to be some form of man-made aircraft. Other sightings often happen during unusual weather events such as lightning storms or strange clouds.

Aeroplanes took to the skies in the early 1900s. These new inventions led to more UFO reports. Humans first began experimenting with rockets and spaceflight in the 1940s and 1950s. That's when interest in UFOs really took off. People found it easier to imagine spaceships from other planets flying to Earth.

Flying saucers

In 1947, a UFO incident grabbed the imagination of people in the United States. Businessman Kenneth Arnold was piloting his small plane above Washington State, USA. He reported seeing nine super-fast objects flying in a V-formation. At first he thought they were military aircraft. But the military later reported it had no planes in that area. Arnold said the objects seemed to skip across the sky, like "saucers" skipping across water.

Newspapers across the United States picked up the story. One news reporter referred to the objects as "flying saucers" because of Arnold's description. The term stuck. Some people **speculated** they might be alien spaceships.

A woman reads a book about UFOs in 1950.

speculate think about or discuss what is uncertain or unknown

The Roswell Incident

In 1947, another UFO incident occurred near Roswell, New Mexico, USA. It has become a classic UFO story.

In early July, a ranch worker found strange **debris** in a field. This was reported to the nearby US Army Air Force base. The base released a statement that a "flying disk" had crashed there. A local newspaper reported the army had captured a "flying saucer". Military officials soon changed the story. A weather balloon had fallen from the sky, they said. As proof, they showed reporters material typical of shiny, silvery weather balloons.

For 31 years the story was mostly forgotten. Then it was shared again in *The National Enquirer*. This newspaper specializes in quirky, attention-grabbing tales. It suggested the Roswell crash had involved **extraterrestrials**. This time the

debris scattered pieces of something that has been broken or destroyed
extraterrestrial life form that comes from outer space

UFO hunters

There are many groups that investigate and study UFOs. They collect reports and photos, and share information. Researchers meet at conferences to talk about their findings. Many members of these organizations believe extraterrestrials have visited Earth. However, no one has yet produced scientific proof.

"Roswell Incident" got a lot more attention. Some UFO researchers said the government covered up proof of alien visitors.

Years later, the Air Force said the crash had not been a weather balloon after all. Instead it came from equipment from a top-secret spy programme. They claimed they had covered up the truth to keep other governments from learning about it. For many people, though, the belief that an alien ship crashed near Roswell has never wavered.

Officer Irving Newton presents debris of a supposed flying saucer in 1947 at Roswell Air Force Base.

FREAKY FACT

Roswell is a tourist destination for people fascinated by UFOs. The town hosts a UFO Festival every July.

The Gorman dogfight

Members of the military are expected to stay cool under pressure. They also have technology that lets them track almost anything that flies. That's why military sightings of UFOs are often taken more seriously.

On 1 October 1948, Lieutenant George F. Gorman was flying his F-51 fighter plane near Fargo, North Dakota, USA. As he prepared to land, something with blinking lights flew past him. He chased it to get a better look. He described the object as a small "ball of light", about 15 to 20 centimetres (6 to 8 inches) in diameter. Other witnesses said they saw a flying light too. Gorman pursued it, reaching speeds of up to 644 kilometres (400 miles) per hour. But he said the object was faster. Finally it shot upwards and disappeared.

Military investigators concluded that Gorman had been fooled by the planet Jupiter or perhaps a weather balloon with lights. Gorman disagreed.

Project Blue Book

In 1952 the US Air Force started Project Blue Book. Its mission was to scientifically investigate UFO sightings. Officials wanted to be sure UFOs were not an unknown threat to the United States. After 17 years the project organizers concluded they had no evidence that extraterrestrials had visited Earth.

Enemy over England?

On 20 May 1957, US Air Force Captain Milton Torres got an urgent order. He was to scramble his fighter jet and chase down a UFO that had appeared on ground **radar**. Thick clouds blocked his view. But the target looked huge on Torres' radar. He was shocked when he was ordered to fire his weapons at the UFO. But it zipped away before he could pull the trigger.

Torres said that afterwards he was warned by a government agent to never talk about the incident. But he shared his story years later. "I think it was an alien spacecraft," he told a reporter.

A photograph from 1957 shows a reported UFO near Holloman Air Force Base in New Mexico, USA.

radar device that uses radio waves to locate objects

Mistaken identities

Most UFO sightings have a reasonable explanation. Here are some of the most common sources of mistaken identity.

Weather balloons

These giant balloons fly to very high **altitudes** to help scientists study weather patterns.

Unusual weather events

Strange cloud formations and lightning can trick people into thinking they have seen UFOs.

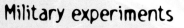

An airman launches a weather balloon

Military experiments

The military sometimes tests experimental aircraft. When spotted, their unusual speed or looks can make them seem like something from science fiction.

FREAKY FACT

The nearest star to our solar system is the star system Alpha Centauri, which is 4.35 light years away. The fastest spacecraft would take about 73,000 years to reach it.

A supercell storm brews over Nebraska, USA.

The Moon and planets

The Moon and bright planets in the night sky have sometimes fooled people into reporting UFOs.

The Hudson Valley UFO sightings

People sometimes go to great lengths to fool witnesses about UFOs. One of the most creative UFO **hoaxes** took place in the mid-1980s in the United States. Thousands of people had spotted huge boomerang-shaped UFOs moving above New York's Hudson Valley. It turned out to be a hoax carried out by a model plane club. They attached lights to their model planes and then flew them in formation.

altitude height of an object above sea or ground level
hoax trick to make people believe something that is not true

CHAPTER 2

THE PUZZLE OF CROP CIRCLES

On an August morning in 2015, English farmer James Hussey woke up to a mystery. Overnight, something had happened in his big field of golden wheat. Parts of it had been pressed down to form a picture of a giant bird. It was an example of a crop circle. When word got out, people flocked to Hussey's farm to see it. No one knew how it had got there.

Crop circles are designs that appear in farm fields. Most people believe they are the work of human artists. However, many crop circle enthusiasts are sure that some have non-human origins. Some blame aliens. Since 1980 more than 10,000 crop circles have been reported in nearly 30 different countries.

The crop circle files

Crop circles come in all shapes, sizes and designs. But most have these details in common:

- they happen in one night
- no clear evidence of who – or what – made them exists
- they appear in fields of grain, such as wheat or barley
- the plant stalks in crop circles are pressed to the ground, not cut

a crop circle found
in Italy in 2014

FREAKY FACT

The study of crop circles is called "cereology". The name
comes from Ceres, the Roman goddess of farming.

Supernatural theories of crop circles

"Croppies" are people who seek proof that crop circles have **supernatural** causes. Here are three theories that croppies have about these **phenomena**.

Theory 1: Wind vortices

In certain conditions strong winds can start spinning. They can even form mini-tornadoes known as vortices. If they touch ground, they may twist plants into a swirled pattern.

Researcher Colin Andrews stands in a crop circle in Wiltshire, England, in 1990.

Theory 2: Earth energy

Invisible magnetic fields criss-cross Earth. This energy is why compasses point north. Different areas, though, have different levels of electromagnetic force. Some croppies believe these forces may cause crop circles to form.

Theory 3: Extraterrestrials

Some people think the patterns mark landing sites for alien spaceships. Others wonder if aliens are sending messages hidden in the designs. They argue some circles have appeared too quickly and been too complex to be the work of humans.

phenomenon very unusual or remarkable events
supernatural magical or not explained by nature

Doug and Dave: Crop circle hoaxers

Starting in 1978, an area in England experienced a rash of crop circles. People gathered to see them. A popular theory was that the crop circles were the work of extraterrestrials.

Meanwhile, a pair of friends was having a good chuckle. Their names were Doug Bower and Dave Chorley. They created the circles and other patterns in the dead of night using a board and their feet. The more they made, the more public excitement grew. Experts stumbled over themselves wondering what caused the mysterious patterns. Doug and Dave made about 200 crop circles, and kept their secret for 12 years.

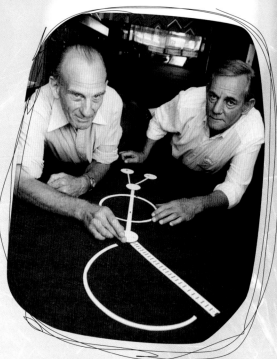

Doug Bower (left) and David Chorley

Examples of crop art

August 2002: Winchester, England. Alien face with computer disc. Measuring 100 metres (330 feet) across.

July 2002: Salisbury Plain, Wiltshire, England. Measuring 230 metres (750 feet) in diameter.

August 2003: West Kennet Long Barrow, Wiltshire, England. A formation of birds in flight.

CHAPTER 3

TALES OF CLOSE ENCOUNTERS

Stories about unexplainable UFOs fire up people's imaginations. Scary tales about being kidnapped by aliens can provoke fear. Scientist and UFO researcher J. Allen Hynek came up with definitions for different kinds of contact with UFOs. He called them "close encounters".

First Kind – viewing of a UFO that seems to be fewer than 150 metres (500 feet) away

Second Kind – feeling or seeing physical effects from a UFO

Third Kind – sighting robots or living beings from a UFO

Fourth Kind – being **abducted** by beings from a UFO

Stories about Close Encounters of the Fourth Kind are the most dramatic – and chilling.

Abduction of the Hills

On the night of 19 September 1961, Barney and Betty Hill were driving home in New Hampshire, USA. After midnight they said they were followed by a bright flying light. The couple arrived home early the next morning. But it seemed about two hours were missing from their memories. Betty started having nightmares about being captured by strange beings.

abduct kidnap
hypnosis trance sometimes used to bring back memories

The Hills tried **hypnosis** to try to recover their lost memories. They described a pancake-shaped flying saucer. They recalled seeing creatures inside it that could communicate without speaking. Barney remembered being terrified when he was dragged on board. They both said they were medically examined. Betty also described having a needle bigger than any needle she'd ever seen stuck in her navel.

The Hills' story became famous and made national news. To many, they seemed believable witnesses to an alien abduction.

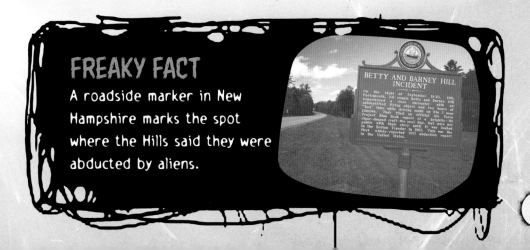

FREAKY FACT

A roadside marker in New Hampshire marks the spot where the Hills said they were abducted by aliens.

the Maine wilderness

The Allagash Waterway Abduction

In 1976, four friends went camping in northern Maine, USA.
While fishing one night, they said they saw an orb-shaped UFO
with flashing lights. It began flying towards them. Panicked,
they paddled their canoe towards shore. The object, though,
overtook them. They woke up several hours later back on
shore. They watched the UFO fly off. But their memories about
what had happened seemed to have been erased.

Afterwards, the group began having nightmares. Under hypnosis they described being abducted. They said they had been beamed aboard the UFO. There, they were examined by strange creatures with long necks and big heads. The four men all passed lie detector tests about the incident. Their similar stories made them more believable.

depiction of the Allagash
Waterway Abduction

Legends of Area 51

In the Nevada desert in the United States, there is a place few people will ever see. UFO researchers refer to it as Area 51. Guards patrol the area to keep anyone from getting near the site. For many years the US military did its best to keep it from even appearing on maps.

To UFO researchers Area 51 is legendary. They wonder whether the place hides evidence of close encounters. Some researchers believe wreckage of the Roswell UFO was sent there. They suspect engineers at Area 51 have taken apart the alien spacecraft to discover how it worked. There have also been rumours that alien bodies and even living aliens have been studied there.

SETI: The Search for Extraterrestrial Intelligence

Some researchers think video or radio broadcasts from other worlds offer our best chance of discovering intelligent life in the galaxy. That is the strategy of the Search for Extraterrestrial Intelligence (SETI) programme. It aims radio telescopes at the sky to search for radio signals from alien civilizations.

In 2013, the US government admitted the base existed. The US Air Force calls the place Air Force Flight Test Center, Detachment 3. It is described as a top-secret airfield for testing spy planes and other experimental aircraft. Some UFO enthusiasts, though, do not trust the story. They think it is part of a government cover-up to hide the truth about alien visitors.

CHAPTER 4

IS THE TRUTH OUT THERE?

UFOs and extraterrestrials have a powerful grip on our imaginations. Our ideas about them are shaped by science-fiction books, films and video games. People are fascinated by the possibility of alien worlds. What would extraterrestrials look like? How would they communicate? What would they eat?

We also wonder whether alien visitors would be friendly or dangerous. Many popular films have explored these hopes and fears. Interestingly, experts note that UFO reports often increase after new films about extraterrestrials are released.

FRIENDLY FILM EXTRATERRESTRIALS

Close Encounters of the Third Kind (1977)	UFO encounters lead humans to first contact with beings from another planet.
E.T., the Extraterrestrial (1982)	An alien explorer is accidentally left on Earth. A group of children work together to help E.T. get home.
Contact (1997)	A scientist makes radio contact with an alien race. She is then sent to meet them.

Close Encounters of the Third Kind won the 1978 Academy Award for best cinematography.

DANGEROUS FILM EXTRATERRESTRIALS

War of the Worlds (2005)	An overpowering force of Martians invades Earth. Science-fiction master H.G. Wells wrote the novel upon which the film is based. The story has been adapted for film and TV several times.
Mars Attacks (1996)	In this comedy Martians attack Earth and the President of the United States. Others must quickly work out a plan of survival.
Independence Day (1996)	Humans face extinction when aliens attack Earth.

In the 2002 film *Signs*, mysterious aliens leave crop circles as messages.

Watching the skies

Almost all reports of alien visitors and spacecraft are based on stories by witnesses instead of scientific research. Investigations indicate these witnesses are unreliable. No one has yet found scientific proof that aliens exist. Still, seeing mysterious objects in the sky can be exciting. It is understandable that people might believe they came from somewhere other than Earth.

There are always wonders to be seen in the night sky. Perhaps one day they will include a spacecraft of extraterrestrial astronauts who have come to say hello.

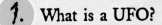

HANDBOOK QUIZ

1. What is a UFO?

a. a spacecraft from
   another planet

b. any flying object that
   cannot be identified

c. any phenomenon that
   cannot be explained

d. a secret military aircraft

2. According to Chapter 1,
UFO sightings increased
after what?

a. the US Air Force began
   searching for them

b. aliens sent messages from
   outer space

c. humans began experimenting
   with aircraft and rockets

d. the invention of the
   flying saucer

3. What are designs called
that mysteriously appear
in farm fields?

a. wind vortices

b. magnetic fields

c. extraterrestrials

d. crop circles

4. "Close Encounters of the
Fourth Kind" refers to what?

a. witnessing UFOs or aliens
   up close

b. being kidnapped by aliens
   from outer space

c. capturing a UFO

d. finding physical evidence
   that UFOs exist

5. According to Chapter 4,
people's ideas about UFOs
and extraterrestrials are
shaped mostly by what?

a. scientific evidence

b. science fiction

c. UFO researchers

d. military reports

Answers: 1-b. 2-c. 3-d. 4-a. 5-b.

GLOSSARY

abduct kidnap

altitude height of an object above sea or ground level

debris scattered pieces of something that has been broken or destroyed

extraterrestrial life form that comes from outer space

hoax trick to make people believe something that is not true

hypnosis trance sometimes used to bring back memories

phenomenon very unusual or remarkable events

radar device that uses radio waves to locate objects

speculate think about or discuss what is uncertain or unknown

supernatural magical or not explained by nature

READ MORE

Non-fiction

Aliens and UFOs (Solving Mysteries with Science), Lori Hile
  (Raintree, 2013)

Crop Circles (Solving Mysteries with Science), Jane Bingham
  (Raintree, 2013)

Have Aliens Visited Earth? (Top Secret), Nick Hunter
  (Raintree, 2016)

Fiction

Amber, Julie Skyes (Curious Fox, 2013)

Can You Survive an Alien Invasion? (You Choose: Doomsday),
  Blake Hoena (Raintree, 2015)

I Am Number Four (Lorien Legacies),
  Pittacus Lore (Penguin, 2011)

INDEX

Allagash Waterway Abduction 22
Area 51 24
Arnold, Kenneth 7

Bower, Doug 18

Captain Milton Torres 11
Chorley, Dave 18
close encounters 20, 24
  First Kind 20
  Fourth Kind 20
  Second Kind 20
  Third Kind 20
crop circles 14, 15, 16–18

films 26, 27

Hill, Barney 20–21
Hill, Betty 20–21
Hudson Valley 13
Hussey, James 14
Hynek, J. Allen 20

Keyhoe, Donald E. 7

Lieutenant George F. Gorman 10

magnetic fields 17
military experiments 12

National Enquirer, The 8
National UFO Reporting Center 29

planets 10, 13
Project Blue Book 10

Roswell Incident 8–9, 24

SETI programme 24

unusual weather events 12
US Air Force, the 4, 9, 10, 11, 25

weather balloons 8, 9, 10, 12
wind vortices 16